I Call

My God

Joe

(further reflections along the spiritual journey)

by Bob Mullin

FORWORD

"I Call My God Joe" (formerly WDGTA)

I wrote "Why Doesn't God Talk Anymore? (and other thoughts along the spiritual journey)" a little over ten years ago. Well, actually what I did was write down where I was at on my spiritual journey at the time. I want to look again at what I wrote then and share with you where I am today on my journey.

 I like the thought that spirituality is not something you get; it's something you live. And faith is not something you have once and for all; it's something you put into practice every day.

Many people thanked me for my book, saying that it expressed how they also felt about the ideas and beliefs that I mentioned. They were glad that they weren't the only ones who felt that way.

Here's what someone said as a review on Amazon.com.

"For all those who question or search for a personal view of God that they can relate to, other than the one they grew up with - this is an amazing book. It does not give one answer. It opens the door to a freedom to find your own vision of God and a relationship with God. It is free from the dogma of any religion yet makes God available to everyone - whether agnostic, atheist or those who are religiously affiliated. Very down to earth! Mr. Mullin says what so many of us think and asks the questions that so many of us ask. A wonderful read!"

This reviewer stated what I was hoping the book would do.

My plan is to present what I said back then and to make comments on what I deeply believe today. After my original reflections I will use the header "*Further Reflections*" and then add my thoughts and prayers. Hopefully it will again encourage others to look at their relationship with their God and grow ever closer to the One Who loves them unconditionally, completely, and passionately. And that gives each one of us a responsibility, not an obligation, but "the ability to respond" to anything that happens to us with love.

The style I used to write the reflections on my journey is meant to encourage you also to reflect on and ponder your thoughts and feelings concerning your religion or spirituality. This is not a book you just read through to get to the end. It is meant more as a meditative experience about your relationship with your God. I suggest you read the book slowly, maybe one chapter at a time. Then think and pray about it.

I Call My God Joe (formerly Why Doesn't God Talk Anymore?)

For

my children

and

their children

Preface to
"Why Doesn't God Talk Anymore"

This book has taken many years to write. It describes the relationship I have had with God and answers to the basic questions of religion and spirituality that I have found along the way.

Some of the questions I have answered are:
Has God stopped talking? Is my God the only God? Which is the true holy mountain? Who's inspired? What's God's name? Who are the Chosen People? Who are God's saints and prophets? Why does God let us suffer?

I spent 12 years in a seminary studying philosophy and theology, including extensive study on the Bible. I left the priesthood after four years of active ministry because I wanted to have my own family and because I could not accept many teaching of the Catholic Church. I attended graduate school where I earned a masters degree in counselor education.

After a failed marriage, I have been happily married for twenty-seven years. Between us we have five grown children. I have been a teacher in a community college for the last thirty-six years.

I share my journey with you because I believe we all walk a similar path. We may call Him by different names, but I believe He is the same loving God. Though many have influenced me along the way, these are my own reflections on what I have learned. It is my belief that we only arrive at the truth through prayer and community.

I want to thank all those who have taught me throughout my life so far. These include my family, my formal teachers, and all those who have touched me either by their books, or words, or actions, or movies, or comments, or questions, or art, or ideas. I do not want to take credit for other people's ideas, though many times I don't know whom to thank. This is neither a dissertation nor a treatise. It is more like a conversation. Your comments and reflections are most welcome.

My prayer is that this might help us to see that we are all one, and that God, by whatever name we call Him, simply loves us and wants us to love one another.

If you would like to share your reactions with me, you can reach me at bob@rjmwritings.com.

Peace and Joy to you.

Acknowledgments

This book would not have been written without the love that God has shown me throughout my life, especially through my family and friends.

I have also been encouraged by those with whom I have shared these beliefs before I ever thought of publishing them. I want to thank Ronnie Vuolo for giving me the final push to publish.

Thanks go to Mindy Ross, my colleague and friend, who first proofread the manuscript. Special thanks go to Karyn M. Hughes, my inspiring little friend, who spent hours and hours editing and revising the manuscript with me to get it just right.

Though I'm sure he's with God already, I want to thank Father George Voilin, my high school junior year religion teacher, who taught me that: "Going to Mass doesn't make you holy; but holy people go to Mass." It is something that I have never forgotten throughout my life.

Introduction

Keep the Faith

"Keep the faith."
That's what people say
when they mean their own faith or belief.
In other words,
     continue to believe
     as I believe.
I say,
     "Keep your faith, but
         let others keep theirs.
     Believe strongly in your faith,
         your way to your God,
            but
     realize that it is your way,
         and not everybody's."
That's OK.
     As a matter of fact,
     I believe it is
     what a loving God would want.

Further Reflections:

I think
      it is extremely important
to remember
      that religion is
      the creation
      of human beings
      like you and me.
Dogma and rituals can be
      changed,
      altered or
      discarded entirely.
God is another matter.
Too many times
      man has invoked
      the authority of God
      to justify their beliefs.

Believers in every religion
      that I am aware of
      have killed
      in the name of their God,
Whom they say is a
      loving,
      merciful,
      compassionate God.
How do we not see

the total incongruity
of such an action?
If you <u>truly</u> believe
in a loving God,
you cannot kill
in His name.
Period!

Also, following certain rituals and rules
do not,
I repeat, do not
make you holy.
What makes you holy is
letting God into your life,
letting His love fill
your heart and soul.
A Jewish friend of mine told me
"Each morning ,
as I put on my yarmulke,
I remind myself that
God is above me
and all around me,
and that I should live this day
in a godly manner,
that I should be
a man of God."

Chapter One

Why Doesn't God Talk Anymore?

I was brought up Catholic,
    and as such was taught that my
    religion was
    the one true religion.
 This made me feel safe,
    though even as a youngster
    I wondered what this meant for
    those others
    who weren't Catholic.
 We were taught that the Bible (the Sacred
Scriptures)
    was the only true word of God,
    and that we should be careful
    not to interpret it
        on our own
        because we might
        misinterpret it.
This confused me because
    if this was God's word to me,
    why couldn't I understand it
    on my own,
    at least as I got older?
However, I was a believer

or perhaps
afraid *not* to be a believer;
so I went along with it and did what
I was told.
We were also taught
not to question things
we didn't understand.
So I tried not to.
It made me wonder.
Later in life I read most of the Bible
Many parts I liked,
but some parts were confusing.
I was told that this was natural,
and that's why we needed
the clergy to explain it to us.
I wasn't talking about the parts
that I didn't understand
because of the way
they were written,
that is, the style or the language, or
that they were translated from the
original languages
in which they were first written.
I had trouble with the parts where
our loving God
was supposed to be helping us
to kill others called the unfaithful.
This and other considerations

have continually bothered me over
the years
and left me
with many unanswered questions.
These thoughts have brought me
to where I am today.
Who are we
or anybody to say
that only these written scriptures
(and the different traditions that go
along with them,
depending on your particular
religion)
are the word of God
and He hasn't said anything
 since then
that is worthy
to be written down and included?
 By the way,
I'm not just talking about the Bible;
 but also the Koran
and any other collection of writings
considered by any religious sect or
denomination or group
to be the only word of God.
I believe that a person
can follow whatever holy writings
he or she wishes to follow,

but I don't think that
your way or my way
is the only way.
I don't see how it can be.
For instance,
for some,
the belief is
that you are only saved
through Jesus Christ.
That leaves out
about 70 percent of the world.
I definitely don't think that
a loving God
would do that.
It seems against His very nature.
One may go through Christ,
another through Buddha,
another through Mohammed,
and so on.
When I was younger, it was thought that
sacred music was provided
by the organist.
The organ
was the only sacred instrument
to provide worship to
the Almighty.
It's the song,
no matter what instrument we use

to worship or sing praise,
     that is important.
It is the prayer
     that is important,
     not the particular words.
We are
     the instruments of God's love.
Who are we
     to say that
     God doesn't talk anymore?
He can talk any time He feels like it.

Think of it this way:
Suppose that,
     when my children started
     kindergarten,
I wrote them several letters about life
     and then went away.
Would I really want them
     to live their lives
     based on what I had written
     when they were young?
No, I wouldn't.
     Unless I told them
       to listen for Him
       every day of their lives.
Also, would I want
     to live my life

only by what I learned
in grade school?
No, I wouldn't.
I'd be unqualified
to make decisions
and live life
as an adult.
I must be constantly
learning
and
growing.

It is the same thing with
my spirituality.
As someone said,
spirituality
is not something you get,
it's something you live.
There's a book about
writing your own *scriptures.*
What a great idea!
Listen to God
in all the ways
He speaks to us
every day;
write them down;
and live by them.

Further Reflections:

When I first titled the book
"Why Doesn't God Talk Anymore?"
    I was really hoping
    that it would be obvious
    that I meant the exact opposite.
Why did organized religions
    put an end to what was
    the Word of God?
Was it a matter of being sure,
    of being secure,
    in the belief
    that these were His words?
It seems that throughout history
    most religious leaders and prophets
    didn't write down what they said.
They believed that
    the spoken word
    was meant to be listen to
    and put into action.
It wasn't about being able
    to quote what they said,
    but to live the message
    that was being delivered.
It was their followers
    who wrote down

what they remembered was said.
I'm sure they meant well.
However I believe I am meant
        to listen to God today and
        put into practice the love
        that He so freely gives
         to us each day.
I must be open to all the ways
        that He reveals Himself to me,
        through whatever means
        He wishes.
I believe God
        puts people in our lives
        that we are to pay attention to
        as if we were responding to Him.
That is how we show our love for Him.
I don't think
        we have to study for years
        or meditate for hours and hours
        to know God's will.
For me, it's very simple.
        God loves me and
        He wants me to love others.
        The only question I have to ask
        myself in any situation is,
        "Am I loving?"

Reflections on Chapter 1

Why Doesn't God Talk Anymore?

Chapter 2

My God Can Beat Up Your God

Throughout history
    there have been
     so many wars,
    so many people killing
    so many other people.
and believing that
    they were doing the right thing.
They really thought
    that their God was on their side.
I saw a poster in a colleague's office once,
      that read something like this:
    "Do you know
     what you are praying for
    when you ask God to win the war,
      to be on your side?"
You are asking Him:
    to maim,
    to blind,
    to blow up,
    to crush,
    to tear apart,
    to kill,
    those who are His children,

as much as *you* are His children.
It's almost saying
my God can beat up your God.
You say that you believe in a loving God,
      who is compassionate and forgiving
      and merciful.
If you believe so,
      why would you ask Him to do all
      those terrible things
          we do in war?
If He is so loving,
      and compassionate,
      and forgiving,
      and merciful,
how can we say that He could do
      such things
      to His children
      whom He loves
      so passionately?
Is it our fear
      that keeps us from seeing
      this terrible contradiction?
I believe the One we believe in,
      as seen in all the different
      sacred scriptures,
tells us: "Fear not."
          "Be not afraid."
          "Peace be to you."

I heard a priest say once that
      the three commandments in the
New Testament are:
      Love your God with all your heart
      and soul.
      Love your neighbor as yourself.
            Be not afraid.
So,
      My God wants to hug your God.
      Or better, my God is your God;
      We just call Him
      by different names.
            We all belong to each other.

Further Reflections:

[On different names we call God,
see the "meditation" on
 "What's Your Name?" in chapter 8.]

I pray every day
      that we will all
      come to realize that
we cannot kill
      in the name of
      a loving God.

Many years ago

33

when I was a teenager
I read a booklet
        by Time/Life magazine
        entitled "The Family of Man."
It had pictures of
        various family groupings
        from around the world.
It demonstrated that my family
        is like your family
        which is like the other guy's family
        and so on.
In other words
        we are all family.
In God's eyes
        we are His one family
        spread throughout the earth
        with our own peculiarities and
        differences, but still one family.
We are all brothers and sisters,
        not just in my country
and not just in your country,
        but in our one world.
 I can't beat you up
        and then claim that
        God gave me the strength to do so.
God gave you and me
        the ability to love.
This gift is sometimes overshadowed

by our insecurities.
I think our fear is that
        there isn't enough to go around and
we are afraid
        we would not get our fair share.
I always wondered about
        sibling rivalry.
Why doesn't each child
        know and accept that his parents
        love him completely and
        love his brother completely
        at the same time.
I have to admit that as a youngster
I was worried about getting my fair share.
I was one of six children
        and a twin to boot.
I also feel more secure
        with people that I know
        than with strangers.
I'm more comfortable with
        those who are like me
        than with those who are
        different from me.
These are very human feelings.
However, I've come to realize
        a long time ago
        that we are one family
        and one world.

Most boundaries
        between countries
        are imaginary lines
        decided upon
        by some people
         to separate
        what is ours
        from what is yours.
But that's all in our head.
        It's not real.
God made us one family
        and gave us
        this one world
        to live in
        together,
        helping each other
        in our daily lives.

I pray that you see that too.

Reflections on Chapter 2:

My God Can Beat Up Your God

Chapter 3:

It's Not the Mountain That's Holy

I go on a retreat twice a year
     with a bunch of men.
We have it at a monastery atop a hill.
Many of the men call it
     "a holy mountain,"
     because it is there
     that they experience
     the presence
     of their God.
I understand why
     they feel this way, but
     I think
 they are emphasizing the wrong thing.
It's not the mountain
     that's holy.
That's just the place where
     we happen to be.
Because
     we are there,
     in that particular place,
     trying to be in contact with God
     and each other,
     it seems holy.

What *is* holy is
    the group of men
    in the presence
        of their God.
It could be
    any mountain,
    or *any* place.
It's not the place that's
        sacred.
It is the event
    of the community
        united in prayer.
Wherever the community is gathered
    God is there
        and therefore
        the community is holy.
In our prayers
    we embody
        the presence
        and holiness
        of God.
It is, therefore,
    definitely,
        not in the name
        of a loving God
    that anyone
        should fight another, or
        kill and maim another

to take over and claim
a certain place
as their sacred right
in which to worship.
How could the Crusades
possibly be considered
God's idea or God's will?
Today the fighting in
the "Holy Land"
by the Christians
and the Jews
and the Muslims
in the name of
their loving God
defiles that land.
God is not present
in the church
or the synagogue
or the mosque
because of the building
or the place.
God is present
when believers gather
in a community of love
wherever
that gathering place is.
A gentle and wise man said that
the day has come

to worship
  not on that mountain
  nor on this mountain,
but
  to worship
  in spirit and in truth.
  as one.

That's what our loving God wants.

Further Reflections:

When we were in the seminary
my friend Tony always said,
  "God is <u>sooo</u> big."
So, why do we think that
  we can contain Him,
  or confine Him to any one place?
When religious leaders consecrate
  a place as a place of worship,
  it is not them
  who make it a holy place.
It is those who come to that place
  to be aware of their God
  that make it holy.
The sense of God's presence
  is what makes it holy.
When I was a priest one of my tasks

was to bless the water
to make it "holy water."
I realized that
it didn't need me to make it holy.
God made the water.
It didn't need my blessing.
And it was the person
who blessed himself with the water
as a ritual of cleansing,
preparing himself,
to meet his God in prayer
that made it holy water.
When we are aware
of the presence of God,
all is holy.
I can pray
wherever,
whenever and
however I choose to pray.
And I can use my own words.

Reflections on Chapter 3

It's Not the Mountain That's Holy

Chapter 4

Suppose I Said I Was Inspired?

What would you think
    if I said that
        I was inspired?
Would you think I was crazy?
    or blasphemous?
    or arrogant?
    or delusional?
Suppose I said that
    someone I knew
    was inspired?
Would you wonder
    how I knew
    or what made me think that?
Let me say clearly
    that *I* don't think
    that *I* am inspired.
That doesn't mean
    that I'm not.
I don't know if I am inspired
    one way or the other.
It is not my place to say.
God can speak

through whomever He wants.
Some people claim that they're inspired,
    that God has revealed things
     to them.
Some people,
    especially the clergy
    and the hierarchy,
    the spiritual leaders,
    of an organized religion
    claim the right to say
    which writings
    are inspired.
Some people say these certain writings
    and *only* these writings
    are inspired,
    and therefore are
        from God.
I know a lot of people who
    for a long time
    have accepted these decisions.
Again,
I don't think it's up to us
    to limit God
        to only so many words.
God can speak
    whenever He wants.
He can reveal Himself
    in any way He wants.

I believe,
        to truly know if
        something is from God,
we have to look at the content
        of the message.
Why do so many scripture scholars
        think they know God's Word
        and so many regular people
        think that God wouldn't talk
        or reveal Himself
        directly to them
        or through someone else to them?
God didn't die
        or go away.
He is still
        with us
        and
        wants us to listen
        to what He's saying
                to us
                today.
That's right.
                    TODAY !!!

Are we listening?

Further Reflections:

Let God himself inspire you through
whatever you are
     reading or
     hearing or
     seeing or
     touching or
     smelling,
for example, through a poem or
     a song or
     a landscape or
     a rain drop or
     a flower.

Listen every day
     with all your senses
but especially
     with your heart
     for what God is saying to you
     throughout your life.
Listen for God
     speaking to you
     through any and every way
     in which He wishes to reach you.
God likes to jump out from behind things
     to help us become
     more aware of His love.

And sometimes,
      He stands right in front of us,
      waiting to be noticed.

Did you ever wonder why
      someone thinks
      the way that they do?
Do you ask yourself,
      "How can they think that
      or do that?"
It just doesn't make sense to us.
The fact is
      we can't understand
      how they think that way
      because we don't think the way that
      they do.
Therefore we can't
      possibly understand
      how God thinks
      because we don't think
      the way He does.
We are very limited in our love,
      whereas He is unlimited.
Do you ever wonder why
      someone gave you
      that gift you got?
We don't understand
      the idea of gift

because many times our gifts
are marked, "RSVP."
But a true gift is freely given out of love.
It doesn't need a reason.
That's why it is a gift.

God's love is like that,
TOTALLY FREE.

Reflections on Chapter 4

Suppose I Said I Was Inspired?

Chapter 5

It's God's Fault – the Differences

Do I pray
     to Allah
     or Jehovah
     or Yahweh
     or Father
     or God?
It's very confusing,
     and I want to get it right.
     I want to be certain.
     I want to be saved.
Who created this mess?
     This confusion?
Some scholars say
it was the Tower of Babel story
     and again blame God
     as punishing mankind.
They say it's because
     they were getting proud,
So God caused them
     to speak different languages
       and be confused.
Maybe God just
     likes variety

and made all the differences
because it was a good idea.
I saw a poster in a local elementary school
that read
"CELEBRATE THE DIFFERENCES."
I think God wrote that.
Look at all the variety,
        all the different flowers,
        all the different trees,
        all the different people,
        all the different cultures,
                all the different everything.
Just sit in a mall
        or on a street corner,
        or beside a road,
and watch all the different people pass by.
Of course God loves
                variety,
                the differences.
That's why He made life that way,
and wants us to enjoy the variety, all of it.
        and we can call Him
                by any name we want,
                as long as
                we let others do the same.

Further Reflections:

The human spirit resides
      in so many different vessels
      of all shapes and sizes and colors.
The size or shape or color is
      of importance only to distinguish
      one beautiful gift from another,
      one beautiful human being from
      another.
We all, each one of us ,
      are a gift from God,
      first to ourselves,
      and then to others.
As St. Paul says in First Corinthians,
      there are different gifts,
      but the same Spirit.
I am not to compare myself with others,
but only
      to be the best "ME" that I can be.
Each one of us is
      a different surface of
      a precious diamond
      that reflects God's love.

Everyone counts.
Everyone makes a difference.
Everyone is needed

to reflect
the all-encompassing breadth
of God's love for us.

By the way,
      don't we enjoy different types of
      foods and different types of clothes
      and different types of entertainment
      and different types of cars?
And could anyone get you
      to change what you enjoy
      to satisfy their needs?
Of course, the truth is
      we like variety in all things and
      God has graciously provided that.
So I think He meant that
      we are to enjoy what we like and
      let others enjoy what they like.

Reflections on Chapter 5

It's God's Fault – the Differences

Chapter 6

God Knows I'm Not A Sinner

"God doesn't make junk."
         You see that saying on
         bumper stickers,
         and on buttons,
         and on posters.
I think that statement
         includes me.
I'm not junk,
         and
         I'm not a sinner.
I don't mean
         that I never sinned.
Of course I have.
         I've sinned.
         I've hurt people.
         I've offended people.
         I've done some terrible
         things in my life
         that I wish I hadn't.
    But I did,
         and I admit it.
         I've sinned.
         But I'm not a sinner.

Let me say it another way.
    I used to be a smoker,
        a heavy smoker,
        several packs a day.
But I wasn't
        just a smoker.
Some people branded me like that:
        "a smoker".
But I am a person,
        a gift from God,
        like we all are.
So though I smoked,
        I wasn't just a smoker.
I am a child of God
        and
        I am a beautiful human being
        because God made me,
        and He doesn't make junk.
    and
        He doesn't made sinners;
He makes human beings,
        who sometimes sin.
So
        I don't believe that we were born
        with original sin.
We were born
        with free will
        and the ability to sin.

I know a lot of people believe that
        Jesus died
        for their sins.
I believe He lived to show us how to live.
        He was killed,
        because He offended
        the people in power,
        who wanted him
        out of the picture.
He also offended a lot of people
        who in their smallness
        couldn't accept the example
        He gave.
So, they crucified Him;
        they hung Him on a cross.
In the same way, Martin Luther King
        and Ghandi,
        and many others
        were killed because of what
        they stood for.
The true sons and daughters of God
        choose to love,
    not because
        of the fear
        of God's punishment,
    but because
        of the love of God.
To accept the love of God

is to accept the choice
to love all others, as He does.

Further Reflections:

Since I first wrote this chapter over ten
years ago, I realize more than ever that
      I am neither devil nor angel.
      I'm a little of both.
      Or maybe a lot of both.
I think of it as living
      with an "open hand" or
      with a "closed hand."
Or to put it another way,
      to think only of myself or
      to think of others.
St. Paul put it in the sense of
      "flesh" vs. "spirit." (Romans)
He meant "to be focused on yourself" vs.
"being focused on others." [See the new
translation of the bible, *The Message* .]
Some refer to it as "your lower self" vs.
"your higher self."
      e.e. cummings says,
      "You need the courage
      to grow up to be
      the person you really are."
We must learn to accept

our human-ness, our imperfection.
It is most important to know that
      we need forgiveness and to know
      that God has already forgiven us.
It is in being forgiven
      that we learn to forgive and
      forgiveness is a divine act,
so it must come from
      an all-loving God through us.
From all those whom I have offended or
hurt or wronged, I ask forgiveness.
And I forgive anyone
      who has offended me.
At the beginning of Mass , the priest says,
"Let us begin by calling to mind our sins."
Why not instead say,
      "Let us begin our celebration by
thinking of all those who have been kind
to us and all those to whom we have been
kind.
      And let us be grateful for
      God's all-encompassing love."
"Eucharist" means "to give thanks."
 We celebrate Mass
      to give thanks to God and
      to be renewed in our commitment
      to share His love with all others.

When we pray, "Lord, have mercy," the
word mercy comes from the Latin
"Misericordia," which is a translation of
the Hebrew, "chesed."
 But chesed means "loving-kindness."
        It means the never-ending love that
        a parent has for a child.
So, at the beginning of
        the celebration of the Eucharist
        we remind ourselves that
        God does love us
        and always will love us.
 Isn't that a better way
        to begin our prayer
        as a community?

Reflections on Chapter 6

God Knows I'm Not A Sinner

Chapter 7

God Knows We Need
Specific Things

Because I am a human being
      with all the characteristics of a
human being,
I need
      concrete or specific things or ways
      to understand and express myself.
God is spirit,
      but He knows
      that I belong to
      time and space.
So it is important to me
      to do things
      in a certain specific time period
      and in a certain specific place.
      and in a certain specific way.
For example,
      I celebrate that I am alive
      on a specific day,
      my birthday.
I show my wife I love her
      by doing specific things,

like bringing her flowers on
Valentine's Day.
I demonstrate my love for my children
with a hug.
I enjoy my friend's company
by having lunch together.
I am body and soul
and need my body
to express my soul,
to express what's in my heart.
It is   *not* the birthday,
nor the flowers,
nor the hug,
nor the lunch
that is important in itself.
It is my way
to express myself.
It is the same thing
with my dealings with my God.
It is how we interact
with our God.
So some worship
on Saturday
in a synagogue,
and some worship
on Sunday
in a church,
or in a mosque.

We're supposed to worship Him
     every day.
We choose
     a certain day
     and a certain place
     to remind us
      to worship Him always.
But it is
     not the specific day
     nor the specific place
     that is important.
It *is* important that we worship Him.
Some celebrate
     Christmas and Easter.
Some celebrate
     Hanukah and Passover.
Some celebrate
     Ramadan.
It is
     not the specific feast
      that is important.
It *is* important that we celebrate our faith.
Some use the Torah
     as a specific spiritual guide.
Some use the New Testament
     as a specific spiritual guide.
Some use the Koran
     as a specific spiritual guide.

These events and books
                  are important to the people
                  who use them.
It *is* important that we have a guide.
It is important that we have a *connection.*

Some come to know God
        through Jesus.
Some come to know God
        through Moses.
Some come to know God
        through Mohammed.
Some come to know God
        through Buddha.
So it is
        not the specific spiritual leader
        that is the *only* way.
It is that He is *a* way.
Some pray
        on their knees;
Some pray
        standing;
        some genuflect;
        some bow;
        some kneel with their heads
        touching the floor;
        some fold their hands;
        some hold their hands open

with palms up;
So it is
not the specific way we pray.
It *is* that we pray.
For us, as humans,
  we need a specific
  thing
  and day
  and place
  and holy day
  and special time
  and written spiritual guide
  and spiritual leader or prophet
  and special prayers,
but these are all
just the different specific ways
  people express their faith in God.
It is not the *way* that is important.
  It is the *expression*
    in some way
    that is necessary.
So I guess that means
  we should let each other
  use his or her own way.
I believe
  that's what God wants.

Further Reflections:

Why do we limit the ways that
        God can reveal Himself to us?
Who are we to say
        that only this way or that way
 is the right way
        for God to interact with us?
Don't we realize that
        we can't make a square circle and
        we can't limit a limitless God?
There is a true story
about a Brother Lawrence,
        a monk who worked in the kitchen
        of a monastery.
That was his job, his vocation,
        because he was not all that smart.
But he knew something
        that most of us miss.
And that is that he knew
        that God reveals Himself to us
        in all things.
Brother Lawrence lived in the awareness
        that he was always
        in the presence of God,
        an all-loving God.

I would like to include here

the introduction to my book,
I'm Asking You. Show Me the Way."

I was on retreat a while back. I go twice a
year, and have been going for over 30
years. This last retreat was different. It
was disappointing in a way. A couple of
my friends didn't make it, one because he
had a wedding to go to and one because
he had died. The retreat master did not
inspire me, so I stopped going to his talks.
I went for a walk in the woods.
When I was in the seminary years ago,
and was having difficulty with my faith,
        I would go for a walk in the woods.
I would just walk,
        asking God to show me the way.
I didn't always get an answer.
As I recall, I didn't get that many answers
from my walks in the woods.
But I did put myself
        in the presence of my God,
        even when I was very confused.
And it worked.
So there I was, walking in the woods,
feeling unfulfilled and empty.
I prayed, *"Show me the way.*
        I'm asking You.

Show me the way."
At one point the sun showed through the
trees. It was so bright I had to shield my
eyes.
That's when I thought of the gospel
passage about the disciples on the way to
Emmaus. [Luke 24: 13-35] It was always
one of my favorite passages.
It reminds me that,
        even when we were unaware of His
Presence, we are not alone.
        He is walking beside us.
Well, during my walk in the woods,
        I realized that, for me, Jesus Christ
        is the one who leads me to my God.
So, I decided I would go through the New
Testament and pick out the words of
Christ that have meant a lot to me over the
years, and still do.
I pray,
"I'm asking You. Show me the way."
I invite you to walk along with me.

Maybe you would find my reflections on
the words of Jesus Christ helpful.
Whether you believe in Him
        as the Son of God or

as a deeply spiritual man who lived
a long time ago,
I think you would find his words
encouraging and inspiring.

Reflections on Chapter 7

God Knows We Need
Specific Things

Chapter 8

A God Called *Joe*

I try to pray to my God regularly.
I try to talk to Him as I live my life.
There have been many days, when I felt
that He wasn't there,
        or if He was,
        He wasn't listening.
I was taught that God was transcendent;
        that He was all-knowing,,
        all-powerful.
When I was young,
     about 10 or 11 years old,
        that was a lot to take in.
I really didn't know what all that meant,
        but I knew it was pretty
        serious.
And there was the thought of a hell too,
        and that was really serious.
I'm not sure that I am recalling
        my thoughts and feelings
        correctly,
     but I think that I thought
        God was really big
        and really far away.

Unfortunately,
      that didn't make sense to me.
So I thought I'd try to get a little closer.
That meant that
            we would have to be more
            familiar with each other.
So, I decided to call him
            Joe.
It was a much friendlier name
         than God
         and not so far away,
         so removed from me.
Of course I didn't tell anyone about this
         because I didn't want to get
         in trouble.
But guess what?
It worked for me.
When I prayed
      I could say,
      "Hey *Joe*, what do you think?"
      or "*Joe*, did you see that?"
      (Of course He did because He was
      all-seeing,
      along with all-everything-else.)
When I went to church, the altar was
      way up there in the front,
      and the priest was
      way up there in the pulpit.

So I used to think of *Joe*
      as sitting up on the rafters
      waving to me,
      and watching over me.
Now,
      if your God was named *Joe*,
      and he hung around with you,
      it would be pretty hard to think of
      Him as a bad guy,
      as someone who was waiting
      for you to screw up so He could
      swoop down
      and beat you up.
Or that He was keeping track of things
      and was waiting to send you to hell.
Of course I wasn't certain
      because the priests
      were saying we were sinners
      and had to go to confession to beg
      God's forgiveness.
Imagine this…
      if *Joe*
      were a loving God
      and wanted to love us completely
      and wanted us to love each other,
      it just didn't make sense
      that He was like they said.
So I held on to *Joe*.

As I grew older, I still had a hard time
        with the way
        a lot of people talked about God,
        especially all that avenging stuff.
Over the years
        I have called Him by many names,
        but I do understand why some
        people say
        He is a God with no name.
For no one name,
        nor word,
        nor attribute
        could describe Him
        completely and fully.
He is
        above all names,
        but He is still the God
        who loves me
        and everyone else,
and sometimes
        He's still
                        Joe.

Further reflections:

Here's another "Meditation" I had while
on a retreat, "What's Your Name?"

WHAT IS YOUR NAME?

I was walking through the woods
*   and I thought I heard someone*
*   speak behind me.*
As I turned around to see who it was,
*   the sun broke through the clouds*
*   and its rays shone through the*
*   trees.*
And there was a brightness
*   on the path in front of me.*
It was as if I was dreaming.

A Voice from within the brightness
*   said, "What do you want?"*
I answered, "What is Your name?

"It is not important
*   what you call Me."*
*   said the Voice,*
*   "Only that you know it's Me."*
I responded,
"But if I don't know Your name,
how do I know it's You when I call?"

"Why do you trust so little?"

the "Voice said.
"I have been with you
since the day you were conceived.
It is My life that lives in you,
        for you are Mine and I am yours."

I said,
        "So it makes no difference
        what I call You,
        only that I do call upon You."
"That's right." said the Voice.
I asked,
 "So do you mind if I just yell,
        'Hey, You! I need You?'"

"But I will already know
        that you need Me,"
        the Voice said.
"It is when you surrender
        to your need for Me
        that you will truly know Me.
And when you do that,
        you will know
        that I have always loved you
        and always will.
I know all that you have done,
        and I have already forgiven you.
It is you who is unaware

of My forgiveness and love.
I have always been by your side.
Just open your heart
    and you will know
    that I am there.
Be not afraid, my little one.
I am known by many names.
So, whichever one you use,
    I will be listening."

For me,
    it's "Joe."

I heard it said that
    the worst thing
that our religion instructors did
    was give us
    certain words to use
    when we prayer,
    like the "Our Father."
I believe
    we are meant
    to talk to our God
    with our own words,
    like we would talk to a friend.
We shouldn't worry about
    using the right words.
All we have to do

is speak from our hearts,
and sometimes,
     not say anything,
     but just sit and
        be quiet.

Maybe you could write Him a letter
     as you would write to a friend.

Reflections on Chapter 8

A God Called Joe

Chapter 9

God's Chosen People

Throughout history
        various groups have claimed
        that they are
        God's "chosen people."
 By this they meant that
        they were the good guys
        and everyone else were
        the bad guys,
        or those other guys.
Some felt
        that it was their job
        to get all the others
        to come to know the truth
        and be converted
        to their way of looking at things
since they were the chosen.
Some actually believed that
        it was their place and
        it was al lright to kill those
        who were not one of them,
        that is, not chosen.
I was one of those

who belonged to a religious group
or church,
who thought that they had
the one true faith,
and that we had to spread
our beliefs so that
others outside could come in
and be saved.
We were all going to heaven
if we did what we were told
were the right things to do.
Like most,
if not all religions,
it was a self-contained system or
way.
To belong and be saved,
you had to do this and that;
and if you didn't,
then you were going to hell
and be damned forever.
And if
you didn't believe
what they said and
how they explained things,
you were definitely lost.
This seemed a silly way,
a scary way,
to be chosen.

Well,
> you were born bad
> and had to be made good
> to become a member,
> and if you didn't,
> you were lost.

So, if you didn't join,
> you were lost,
> and if you joined and
> didn't keep the rules and
> regulations,
> you would still be lost.

This is what
> God's chosen people said.

Then,
> I didn't want to belong.

But then what was I to do if
> I chose not to be
> with God's chosen people?

I came to see
> that it didn't make sense.

To be
> the chosen people
> of an all-loving God
> was not like
> belonging to a select club
> whose members
> were better than everyone else,

and whose leaders
were better than that.
Somewhere
along the way,
the understanding of being
God's chosen
got all screwed up.
I think it was
because people were fearful
and wanted to feel safe;
so they got together
with a bunch of other people
and started to tell themselves
that they were the ones
who were right,
and started to make rules
to keep them right,
and therefore safe.
They were right and safe
because they believed in their God
who told them
they were right and safe.
If the thinking here is getting confusing,
it's not you.
To belong to a religion becomes
a self-contained safety net,
that goes against the very thing
that that religion was meant to be.

Let me explain it this way.
To be one of
      God's chosen people
      is an unbelievable gift
          and responsibility.
You are not chosen
      because you are better
      than others.
The fact that you are chosen
      does not make you better than
      others.
To be chosen does not give you the right
      to look down on others.
To be chosen does not guarantee you
      a place in heaven.
To be chosen means
      to be aware of
      the awesome fact
      that
      God loves you.
      He loves you passionately
      and not just you,
          but everyone
(though most people don't believe this).
To be chosen,
      means to be filled
      with the joy of faith,
      to believe that

you are loved
by this awesome God,
and to want to tell others about it.
You do this best
by loving others,
by responding to God's love,
by letting God's love flow
in you,
and through you.
Consider this…
It's like being a teenager in love,
who finds out that
the girl he cares for cares for him,
and he feels this uncontrollable joy
and wants to tell everyone
and love everyone.
It's an overflowing wonderfulness.
It has nothing to do with
having deserved God's love.
You aren't loved
because you deserve it;
you're loved
because you're loved.
God loves us
before
we do anything
to deserve it;
and,

once we accept this love,
our response is
to love others.
Think of someone
you love.
Now, if I were to ask you
why you love that person,
you would probably hesitate,
and then say because you do.
If I pushed you for specifics,
you would probably say because
he's kind,
or generous,
or smart,
or whatever.
Aren't all those things we say
just excuses
as to why you love
your spouse or friend?
Love doesn't need a reason.
You love him because
you love him;
and that's the nature of
love---a free overflowing.
That idea or way of expressing it
helps me
to understand God's love.
He just loves us,

and
　　　He does it first,
　　　　　unconditionally,
　　　　　　　and without limit.
This is the gift
　　　of being
　　　one of God's chosen,
　　　to be aware of His love
　　　and to share it with all,
　　　that's all,
　　　　　and
　　　I really mean
　　　　　all others.

Further Reflections:

Let me explain being "chosen"
　　　in the following manner.
I am a recovering alcoholic.
By the grace, the free gift of God,
I don't feel the need to drink anymore.
I don't take any credit for my sobriety. I
do take the responsibility to stay sober.
I tried many times to get and stay sober.
By myself I couldn't do it.
Then, one day I said,
　　　"I can't do it!"
And God took that as my prayer.

I surrendered
      and He lifted me up.
I know with all my heart
      that this was and is
      a totally free gift.
I did nothing to deserve it.
It's like love.
You don't deserve to be loved;
      you are just loved.
That's a hard concept to grasp when so
many people tell us we have to do
something first before we are enough,
before we can be loved.
So, I have been "chosen" by God to live a
sober life.
 I was not better than others
      to be chosen.
It does not make me better than others
      to be chosen.
God gave me this free gift so that
      I can freely give to others.
It's that simple.
All I need to do is
      to accept with great gratitude
      this free gift,
      and live my life doing the best
      that I can do.
When I was in the active ministry,

I gave a sermon on "reserved seats."
I told everyone in the church that we had
        reserved seats in heaven.
There was nothing that we had to do
        to get them.
            They were already given to us.
 So then the question is
        "now what do I do?"
If I don't have to do anything
        to be "saved," then what?
And the simple answer is
                        "to love."

Reflections on Chapter 9

God's Chosen People

Chapter 10

God Doesn't Want Us To Wait

So many people
      are waiting,
      expecting,
      hoping for,
      looking forward to,
      searching for
      the One who is to come
            or
      the One who is to return.
Maybe that's why
      we are missing Him.
He's already here;
      He's with us now.
He always has been,
      and always will be.
God
      is a God
      of the "here and now."
We must stop waiting.
Perhaps the real question is,
      "why are we waiting?"
Most faiths say that
      God is present.

So let's live as if
     we *really* believe
     that God is present.
I was once asked
     if I were guaranteed
     a seat in heaven,
     what then would I do?
     How would I live?
In other words,
     I didn't have to do anything else
     to gain it;
     I already had
     a reserved place in heaven.
So, now what?
     If "being good" is not
     a matter of ensuring a place
     in heaven, that is,
        of being saved,
then what is the point of being good.
Living a virtuous life is a matter
     of living heaven now,
     of living in the presence of God,
     who is a loving God.
Living a virtuous life starts
     with the belief that
     the One is already here,
     and that
     that One lives in each of us,

and that His love should flow
through each of us
    today,
    right now.
Maybe we have to think of the world
    as one big place of worship,
where we are aware of
    God's loving,
    abiding presence;
where we realize that
we are all of the same family,
that we are all brothers and sisters,
that no one is left out,
so no one has to be afraid,
as if there's not
    enough of God
    for everyone.
There's plenty of God.
In our fear
    we clench our fists,
    instead of opening our hands,
    and miss the love of God
    bouncing all over the place.
So let's not wait
    any longer
    for there's nothing
    to wait for.
He's already here.

His presence is
        His present
                to us;
our awareness and love is
        our present
                to others.

Further Reflections:

Sometimes I don't want to accept
        the miracles I see in my life.
Because if I do,
        then I have to accept all as miracle,
        that is, as a sign of God's all-loving,
        all-abiding presence.
 I once heard in a sermon the priest
explain it this way.
We aren't always aware of the presence
        of the sun in the sky.
It might be a cloudy day or a rainy day.
Or maybe we're just caught up
        in our own little world.
But when the warmth of the sun
        touches our face,
        we are grateful for the fact that
        there is a sun.
So, in the same way,
we are not always aware of

God's presence
. But when He reveals Himself
        in a gentle breeze or
        through the soft touch of a loved
        one, we are grateful that He is there.
I heard it said that if you don't feel the
presence of God,
        who moved?
Don't wait until tomorrow
        to tell someone you love them.
Tell them today, right now.
        And you will be "the hand of God"
        reaching out to them
            and offering them comfort.
When you ask,
        "God, are You there?"
The answer is,
        "Yes!"

Reflections on Chapter 10
God Doesn't Want Us To Wait

Chapter 11
God's Saints And Prophets

According to Funk & Wagnall's Standard
Desk Dictionary,
     "a saint is a holy or godly person",
and
     "a prophet is one who delivers
     divine messages
     or interprets the divine will."
According to certain religions,
     there are only a few of these and
     the rest of us come up wanting.
I don't understand why
     religious leaders feel
      they must limit the number of
     saints and prophets
     to just a few and
     that's very, very few,
      only one or two
     every couple of hundred years.
No wonder
     so many believers feel
       unworthy of sainthood and
     that they are "not enough."
It's a very exclusive club
     and the ones holding the keys

don't seem to understand
the God they're talking about.
A saint is
a holy or godly person, that is,
someone who tries to imitate
the love of God
in his or her own life.
A prophet is
one who delivers divine messages,
the most important message being
that God loves us.
According to various religious groups,
each of these
two must be accompanied by
signs, or miracles,
to be considered authentic.
Is not compassion a sign of God?
Is not forgiveness a sign of God?
Is not kindness a sign of God?
Is not sacrifice a sign of God?
Is not love a sign of God?
Are not all the expressions of love,
that is, signs of God?
I believe
there are thousands,
no…millions,
of saints and prophets,
and we're just not paying attention

or we're looking for
the wrong things.
Here's a partial list for you to consider
and add to:
+ the mother who cradles her
hurting child
+ the father who works several jobs
to feed his family
+ the reporter who volunteers in
the soup kitchen
+ the daughter who takes care of an
ailing mother
+ the boy who shares his lunch at
school
+ the girl who helps her little sister
+ the co-worker who listens to your
problems
Don't these people demonstrate
the love of God?!
+ the laborer who gives 100% to
his job
+ the teacher who respects and
cares for his or her students
+ the friend who shares your loss
of a loved one
+ the spouse who walks the road of
life with you

+ the stranger who stops to change your flat tire

+ the doctor or nurse who tends to your pain

+ the cashier who smiles and asks about your day

Aren't these messengers of God's love?!

+ the firefighter or police officer who gives his life in the line of duty

+ the accountant who is honest in his life and in his work

+ the dishwasher who toils for his family

+ the person who says hello when you're feeling all alone

+ the school psychologist who bears the hurt of her pupils

+ the recovering alcoholic/drug addict who is kind to others

+ the person who forgives your transgressions

God's saints and prophets
                are *everywhere*
                whispering
                His loving kindness
                and
                proving that He is here
                 with us.

Further Reflections:

I don't feel the need to add
     any other examples to the list.
Maybe you can take a few moments
     to think about those
     who have touched your life
     in a caring, loving way.
And, while you're at it, be grateful for
     all the opportunities you have had
     to influence other people's lives in
     a positive way, through all the
     experiences of life.
We are all called to be holy.
     That means to love one another.
I like the Dalai Lama's comment:
     "My religion is kindness."

Reflections on Chapter 11

God's Saints And Prophets

Chapter 12

A God Called *Sarah*

When I spoke of
      calling my God
         Joe,
I was saying what I did
      to feel closer to my God.
I did not mean any disrespect
       to anyone else
      and hope none was taken.
I especially did not mean to say
      that He could only be,
         a male God.
A friend of mine
      refers to her God
         as *Sarah*,
      and that's great.
What's important
      is what makes you feel comfortable
      with your God.
"God, our Mother,"
      is as correct as
      "God, our Father."
When I refer to God
      in my writing as Him,

I realize that He is not really
      of the male gender.
Actually He is
      neither male
      nor female.
I did not want to use the term "He/She."
Maybe that's why some call God
      the "God with no name."
God is a spirit,
      and not limited
      by physical time and space.
We are.
      So, we have to pick something
      by which to call Him.
It is difficult
      to describe Him
      without using human terms,
      though we realize
      He far exceeds
        our descriptions.
It is like having
      a picture of a loved one
       in our wallet.
We do not love the picture,
      even if we kiss it;
it is simply a constant reminder
      of the one we love.
Whichever name

makes us feel close to God
is the name we should use.
However, we should not limit others
to use the same name.
They should use their own.
In no way
can God ever be contained,
and if we try to do so,
then we are not talking about
the true God.

Further Reflections:

In Chapter 8, "A God Called Joe,"
I included my meditation on
"What's Your Name?"
The problem of giving God a name
is twofold.
First, we need a specific name
by which to call God.
And second, when we name something we
have the tendency to think that we control
it. Well, in reality all we can control is
ourselves and maybe not even that
completely.
God is a God of transcendence
and a God of Immanence
at the same time.

He is within us
and so far beyond us
simultaneously.
God is a mystery in the sense that
we are to be open
to any and all the ways
He wishes to reveal Himself to us.

Ubi caritas et amor, Deus ibi est.
Where charity and love prevail,
there is God.

We can't really describe the wind.
We can only notice
its presence in all its forms.
Maybe , no, truly, God is Spirit
and cannot be contained
any more than we can
hold the wind in our hands.

"Be still, and know that I am God."
Psalm 46:10

Reflections on Chapter 12

A God Called *Sarah*

Chapter 13

God Made Our Bodies Beautiful

God made us,
      male and female.
  He created us,
      and saw that we were good.
That includes our bodies,
      not just our minds and souls,
          but every part of us.
Because He made
      our bodies beautiful,
      then it follows that
      physical love is
          beautiful and
          part of His plan.
I don't understand why
      so many religious leaders talk as if
       God didn't want us to have
      physical pleasure
      when we demonstrate our love.
If He didn't,
      He wouldn't have created us
          the way He did.
(In the story of the Garden of Eden,
      it is a sin of "wanting to know",

not a sin of a sexual nature.)
Though I believe that
 celibacy is one way to love God,
 it is not the *only*
 nor the better way;
  it is simply one way.
In the Catholic religion
 marriage is
 as much a sacrament as
  priesthood;
both are sacraments, or signs,
  of the love of God
  and the infusion of His grace.
(Though that isn't the way it is often
understood in the Catholic Church.)
It is the spiritual and physical union
 of two people
  that is
 the content of love and devotion.
Even though some have misused
 the physical aspect,
 that doesn't make it bad of itself.
I once heard
 a priest describe heaven as
  an eternal orgasm.
 What a fantastic concept!
 What a way to describe
 the joy of being

in the presence of God!
After all,
       God is
       passionately
       in love with us,
       that is, full of passion,
       or ardently and
        intensely loving us
       with His entire Being.
Shouldn't we love
       each other
       in the same way,
       with the totality
       of who we are?

"And God saw that it was good."

Further Reflections:

Let me repeat here some comments
I made in "Further Reflections"
in Chapter 6.
When St. Paul talked about
       "flesh" vs "spirit," he did not mean
       "body" vs "soul."
       The Message, the new translation of
       the Bible, puts it this way,

"being focused on self" vs
"being focused on others."
So he was not condemning physical love.
God made us male and female and
"saw that it was good."
Obviously we are meant
to enjoy the pleasure
in giving ourselves completely
to each other.
I believe that God meant us
to unite and consecrate our love
in an intimate physical way.
We are to become "one."
Like anything, however,
physical intimacy can be abused.
And, to me, that is a terrible wrong.

One last thought:
there's nothing like a caressing hug.

Reflections on Chapter 13
God Made Our Bodies Beautiful

Chapter 14

God Knows Our Pain

Throughout the centuries,
    spiritual leaders and others
    have tried to explain
    why people suffer,
    why there is suffering,
        why some people suffer and
    others seem not to.
I do not intend to provide
    a satisfactory answer
        to this ongoing question,
    but to share with you
        how you might handle
        your own suffering.
I like the comment that goes,
    "If I knew the answer to that,
        I'd be God."
I don't understand
    a lot of things
    and I wish I did.
It would make it easier to handle.
Give me a reason
    why I'm suffering
    and I'll deal with it.

We *can* give meaning
        to suffering,
        for example,
        as a means of connecting
                with others,
        as a means of offering up
                something for others.
Each of us has
        our own path to follow,
        and some paths seem
        easier than others.
However, I only have one life to live
                and it's mine.
I have to live it;
        no one can live it for me.
I have to bear
        my own pain and suffering.
Because I am blessed,
        I do not have to bear it
                alone.
I have my family and friends,
        and I have my God.
My God doesn't explain
        everything to me,
        but He is with me
        in whatever I am going through.
I have trouble with social injustice,
        and with people starving to death,

and especially with little children
being sexually abused.
God created us
and we are capable of
so much goodness;
and we are capable of
so much evil.
We can give life and heal others,
physically and spiritually;
and we can cause death and wound others,
physically and spiritually.
I do believe that
good can come out of bad,
that we can overcome
whatever happens to us,
even things that violate
our very beings.
There are those
who have shown us the way,
who have shared their hurt
and their courage,
and their victory.
For example…
+ the mother, who lost a young
child to illness, who consoles other
women after their similar loss

+ the young man in the hospital
dying of cancer, who brings
laughter to fellow patients
+ the woman, who was raped as a
child, who now uplifts others
through her encouragement
+ the recovering alcoholic who
caused so much damage and grief
while drinking, who today helps
many others to stop drinking and to
lead caring and fruitful lives
+ the woman, who lost her young
husband in a tragic accident at a
young age, and the man, who failed
in his first marriage, who have
celebrated 27 years
as a loving and caring couple
I do believe that
we have been given
the tools of
compassion and forgiveness
to go *beyond*
the terrifying experiences
in our lives.
I do believe that
no matter what may happen to me
God loves me
and is with me

and will hold me in His hands,
and that He wants us
              to help one another
              with the divine life
              that He instills in us.
I know that
              suffering is part of life.
I don't know the answers,
              but
                He does
                      and I trust Him.

Further Reflections:

I must start off with what I say
in conversations about suffering.
 "If it's happening to you,
       I am very philosophical;
 if it's happening to me,
       I am a whining wimp."
I don't mean that I take someone's
suffering lightly. Not at all!
 I believe I have had a fairly easy life,
though I've been through a divorce and I
am a recovering alcoholic.
So many other people that I know have
had to bear terrible suffering, such as the

death of a young child or a life-changing
sickness.
I admire the courage with which
　　　these people live their lives.
I'm not sure that I would have that kind of
courage.
I wrote this poem when I was feeling the
pain of divorce.

I was lost in the forest of hurt,
　　　thinking of broken promises
　　　and betrayed confidences,
when a sparrow with a broken wing
hobbled through the trees and
　　　I followed him towards tomorrow.

At the time I saw a priest friend of mine
and I said to him that I was getting a
divorce and was planning to tell him all
the hurt I was feeling.
He beat me to the punch and said,
　　　"What have you learned from it?"
I wanted to hit him because I wanted him
to feel sorry for me and console me. But I
realized that he asked the right question.
Some believe this life is just an illusion
and that's their answer to the question of
suffering.

I believe this life is real and
        suffering is just part of it.
A lot of people say that
        life is not fair.
Well, I say
        love is not fair.
Love does not seek justice,
        but compassion.
Love does not judge,
        but shows mercy.
Love needs no reason to do what it does.
It is simply love's nature to be completely
accepting and forgiving.
I really don't understand suffering
        any more than I understand love.
When I am loving or being loved,
        all questions go away and
        the moment becomes everything.
For me it comes down to a matter of trust.
I trust my God
        that He will be by my side
        no matter what happens.
        And when I do that, all is OK.
P.S. Sometimes we have to sit with the
pain. This was told to me by my friend
whose name is Faith. Quite a statement!

Reflections on Chapter 14

God Knows Our Pain

Chapter 15

God's Two Special Gifts

I believe
      we have been given
      two special gifts
      with which to live our lives.
Both are
      equally important.
In fact, one
      without the other
      causes an uneasiness,
      an incompleteness,
      an inability to be at peace.
Together,
      yes,
      by complementing each other,
            we truly live.
The first is
      the gift
      of the need to be loved;
the second is
      the gift
      of the need to love.
The world seems to emphasize
      the first, being loved
      and forgets, or misplaces

the second, loving.
These two gifts really belong
        together;
The one gift
        is not complete
        without the other.
We know
        we desperately
        need and want
        to be loved,
but
        we have difficulty admitting it
        because then
        we become vulnerable.
To be loved for ourselves,
        we have to be willing
            to reveal our flaws
            (which we all have).
That scares us
        because
        if we take the risk to show someone
        who we really are,
        and we are rejected, then
                what do we do?
It is only when
        I reveal my true self,
        with all the nicks and scars,
        all the fears and troubles,

that
I truly authenticate myself,
and authenticate
and love you.
The world is always telling us
we're not enough;
We're not
tall enough
or thin enough,
or smart enough
or pretty enough.
We *are enough*,
right now,
just as we are.
It is exactly in being ourselves,
with all our limitations,
that we become enough.
By loving
and accepting ourselves,
we transcend all
that keeps us from ourselves.
Think of a moment when
everything felt so peaceful,
so serene,
so together.
At that moment,
you sensed,
you knew that everything,

I mean everything,
was OK.
You were one
　　with the world,
　　and everything in it;
　　and the world was one
　　with you,
　　just as you are.
These moments
　　are windows to reality.
The rest is just
　　distraction.
When we give of ourselves,
　　of our *true* selves,
　　we give others
　　　　the opportunity
　　　　to love us;
　　and that helps them
　　　　to fulfill the other gift ---
　　　　the need to love.
The lack
　　we feel
　　in our lives
　　is that
we do not love enough;
that is the missing part.
It's not that
　　we need more;

it's that
>we have to give more.
We do have our imperfections, but
>we also have been given,
>each one of us,
>certain talents,
>or skills,
>or abilities,
>that make us special.
These gifts
>have been given to us
>>not for ourselves,
>>but for others.
It is not important
>what talents others have.
Those are
>their gifts.
We all have to use
>our own gifts.
It is in doing so
>that we love,
that we fulfill
>our need to love.
Each of us has
>an unbelievable part
>to play in this life.
Each of us
>is meant

to make a difference.
Each of us
    has the ability
    and the opportunity
    to enhance others' lives.
When you use the gift
    of who you are,
and I use the gift
    of who I am,
we touch each other
    in a positive way;
and that is
    the real gift of life.
Some people affect others
    like a powerful storm
    or a rushing river;
but don't underestimate the effect
    of the gentle breeze
    or the quiet whisper.
Each of us has
    a sacred calling.
    to be who we are,
    and to use the talents given to us,
not to change the world,
    but
    to love the world,
and in doing so
    the world will change itself.

Further Reflections:

This chapter was actually the talk I gave at
graduation the year that I retired from full
time teaching. (Thankfully, I am still
teaching part time and still enjoying it.)
When I was thinking about
        what I wanted to say,
I needed to come up with something
        that I thought would be
        an important life lesson
but that could also be said within
        a three to five minute time frame.
In a way I guess
        it's my philosophy of life.
A friend said to me a long time ago that
all she wanted to do in life
        was love
        and be loved.
And that was my message to the students.
Loving and being loved is
        what life is all about.
Did you ever notice that you don't feel
lonely when you are loving,
        when you are thinking of others?

As I said in my talk, we need to exercise
our need to love more often.
And when we do,
        our hearts grow bigger and bigger.
        Love is the only thing that becomes
        more when it is given away.
One last thought comes from a poster I
use to have on my wall in my room.

WE ARE HERE
NOT TO PASS JUDGMENT,
BUT TO LOVE.

P.S. No matter what happens to me,
        I always have the capacity to love.

Peace & Joy to you all,
                                    Bob

Reflections on Chapter 15

God's Two Special Gifts

Chapter 16

Prayer

I wanted to add this chapter
on prayer because it is a question
that so many people ask.
How do I pray?

For those of the Christian faith,
here is an example of how to pray
        the Our Father.
I understand that some scripture scholars
say that when Jesus gave
        the Our Father to His disciples,
He meant it more as an outline
        of how to prayer.
 So I include here
        a meditation on this prayer.

Our Father.
We can only say it together,
        whether we are physically alone or
        in community with others.
God belongs to everyone and we should
always pray united in spirit to our brothers
and sisters in God's one family.

Who art in Heaven.
The kingdom of heaven is within you.
We share life with each other.
When we love one another,
      God is present.

Hallowed be thy name.
We honor God
      when we support one another,
 when we show kindness and compassion.

Thy Kingdom come.
We help the Kingdom along
      when we live our lives
      with one another in mind.

Thy will be done.
God's will is
      that we love one another.

On earth as it is in heaven.
When we are aware of God's love,
      heaven is already here.

Give us this day our daily bread.
It is one day at a time.
      Just for today.

Forgive us our trespasses.
He already has,
      and always will.
Nothing can keep us from His love.

**As we forgive those who trespass
against us.**
As God has forgiven and loves us,
we should do so for ourselves
      and each other.

And lead us not into temptation.
Even when tempted
      we are not alone.
God is with us.

But deliver us from evil.
We have been delivered from our
selfishness and self-centeredness.
      We have been freed.

**For Thine is the kingdom and the
power and the glory,
forever and ever. Amen.**
      So be it.

I heard a priest once say
      that it was a mistake
      to be given certain words
      to use in our prayer,
as if these were the only "right' words.
Prayer is
      talking to God
      as we would talk to a friend,
      and we listen to Him in confidence.
In my opinion,
      it's more a matter
      of being aware of His Presence
      and basking in his love.

 I have a suggestion.
      Why don't you write
      a love letter to your God?
      Or go for a walk
         in the woods with Him.
      Or sing a song to Him.
      Or tell Him a story.
      Or sit on the beach
         and listen to Him.

Again, I wish you peace & joy. Bob

If you have any comments or thoughts
you would like to share, you may reach
me at bob@rjmwritings.com

If you are interested,
check out my other books:

A Flickering Candle: Chris's Story

To Touch a Life

I'm Asking You. Show Me the Way.

About the Author

Bob Mullin has formal degrees in philosophy, theology and counseling. This includes extensive study of the Bible and an examination of other religions.

He spent twelve years in the seminary in preparation for the priesthood. Bob was assigned to a parish in South Ozone Park, New York, where he served his parishioners for four years.

Bob presently lives with his wife in Middletown, New York, where he is a professor in the Business Management Department at Orange County Community College.

He shares the story of his experiences with his faith, using personal anecdotes in poetic form to illustrate how God worked in his life. He explores various aspects of the doubts, fears, and perplexities he has experienced as a believer in various life situations. His writing is honest and self-disclosing. The personal, poetic format of the book suits his reflections on faith and the nature of God.

Made in the USA
Columbia, SC
29 May 2018